THIS BOOK BELONGS TO

NAME:
_____

ADDRESS:
_____
_____
_____

Phone Number:
_____

Favorite Scripture:
_____
_____
_____
_____

The 5 Minute Christian Journal

Journaling stimulates the mind. It increases happiness, helping you to develop a more optimistic approach to each day of your life so that you can build stronger more meaningful relationships, and find joy and peace in the simple things in life.

When journaling is used for self- reflection and improvement, it can help you to explore and understand yourself better, so that you can grow personally and become the best version of yourself.

The first few minutes of each day are vital in setting the tone for the rest of your day. Therefore, taking this time to write in your journal, to meditate, pray and practice gratitude and appreciation for life's blessings is extremely important.

This journal will help you to do just that. It allows you to start each day with an inspirational Bible scripture verse, a prayer of gratitude and thanksgiving and positive affirmations.

It will also help you to reflect on good things throughout your day, ensuring that you end your day on a positive note.

At nights you will evaluate your day and detail how you will improve for tomorrow.

Psalm 117

1. O praise the LORD,
all ye nations:
praise him, all ye people.

2. For his merciful kindness is
great toward us:
and the truth of the
LORD endureth forever.
Praise ye the LORD.

Date: _____

"The steadfast love of the LORD never ceases; his mercies never come to an end; they are new every morning; great is your faithfulness." *(Lamentations 3:22-23)*

Dear God; Today I am most grateful for:

What would make today a great day for me?

Today's Affirmation: I am...

What is the most amazing thing that happened today?

How will I make tomorrow better?

Date: _____

"Trust in the LORD with all your heart, lean not on your own understanding. In all your ways acknowledge him, and he will direct your path." (Proverbs 3:5-6)

Dear God; Today I am most grateful for:

```
┌─────────────────────────────────────────────────┐
│                                                   │
│                                                   │
│                                                   │
└─────────────────────────────────────────────────┘
```

What would make today a great day for me?

```
┌─────────────────────────────────────────────────┐
│                                                   │
│                                                   │
│                                                   │
└─────────────────────────────────────────────────┘
```

Today's Affirmation: I am...

```
┌─────────────────────────────────────────────────┐
│                                                   │
│                                                   │
│                                                   │
└─────────────────────────────────────────────────┘
```

What is the most amazing thing that happened today?

_____

_____

_____

_____

How will I make tomorrow better?

_____

_____

_____

_____

Date: _____

"The name of the LORD is a strong tower; the righteous runs into it and is safe."
(Proverbs 18:10)

Dear God; Today I am most grateful for:

What would make today a great day for me?

Today's Affirmation: I am...

What is the most amazing thing that happened today?

_____
_____
_____
_____

How will I make tomorrow better?

_____
_____
_____
_____

Date: _____

"I have set the LORD always before me; he is at my right hand, I shall not be shaken."
(Psalm 16:8)

Dear God; Today I am most grateful for:

[ ]

What would make today a great day for me?

[ ]

Today's Affirmation: I am...

[ ]

What is the most amazing thing that happened today?

_____
_____
_____
_____

How will I make tomorrow better?

_____
_____
_____
_____

Date: _____

"Even though I walk through the valley of the shadow of death, I will fear no evil, for you are with me; your rod and your staff, they comfort me." **(Psalm 23:4)**

Dear God; Today I am most grateful for:

What would make today a great day for me?

Today's Affirmation: I am...

What is the most amazing thing that happened today?

_____
_____
_____
_____

How will I make tomorrow better?

_____
_____
_____
_____

Date: _____

"Be strong, and let your heart take courage, all you who wait for the LORD!"
(Psalm 31:24)

Dear God; Today I am most grateful for: ☀

```



```

What would make today a great day for me?

```



```

Today's Affirmation: I am...

```



```

What is the most amazing thing that happened today? ☽

_____
_____
_____
_____

How will I make tomorrow better?

_____
_____
_____
_____

Date: _____

"The LORD of hosts is with us; the God of Jacob is our fortress." **(Psalm 46:7)**

Dear God; Today I am most grateful for:

```
┌─────────────────────────────────────────────┐
│                                               │
│                                               │
│                                               │
└─────────────────────────────────────────────┘
```

What would make today a great day for me?

```
┌─────────────────────────────────────────────┐
│                                               │
│                                               │
│                                               │
└─────────────────────────────────────────────┘
```

Today's Affirmation: I am...

```
┌─────────────────────────────────────────────┐
│                                               │
│                                               │
│                                               │
└─────────────────────────────────────────────┘
```

What is the most amazing thing that happened today?

_____
_____
_____
_____

How will I make tomorrow better?

_____
_____
_____
_____

Date: _____

"Cast your burden on the LORD, and he will sustain you;
he will never permit the righteous to be moved." (Psalm 55:22)

Dear God; Today I am most grateful for:

What would make today a great day for me?

Today's Affirmation: I am...

What is the most amazing thing that happened today?

_____
_____
_____
_____

How will I make tomorrow better?

_____
_____
_____
_____

Date: _____

"He only is my rock and my salvation, my fortress; I shall not be shaken." **(Psalm 62:6)**

Dear God; Today I am most grateful for:

[ ]

What would make today a great day for me?

[ ]

Today's Affirmation: I am...

[ ]

What is the most amazing thing that happened today?

_____
_____
_____
_____

How will I make tomorrow better?

_____
_____
_____
_____

Date: _____

"The LORD is my strength and my song; he has become my salvation." (Psalm 18:14)

Dear God; Today I am most grateful for:

_____

What would make today a great day for me?

_____

Today's Affirmation: I am...

_____

What is the most amazing thing that happened today?

_____
_____
_____
_____

How will I make tomorrow better?

_____
_____
_____
_____

Date: _____

"Glad songs of salvation are in the tents of the righteous:
The right hand of the LORD does valiantly." (Psalm 118:15)

Dear God; Today I am most grateful for:

```
┌─────────────────────────────────────────────┐
│                                             │
│                                             │
│                                             │
└─────────────────────────────────────────────┘
```

What would make today a great day for me?

```
┌─────────────────────────────────────────────┐
│                                             │
│                                             │
│                                             │
└─────────────────────────────────────────────┘
```

Today's Affirmation: I am...

```
┌─────────────────────────────────────────────┐
│                                             │
│                                             │
│                                             │
└─────────────────────────────────────────────┘
```

What is the most amazing thing that happened today?

_____
_____
_____
_____

How will I make tomorrow better?

_____
_____
_____
_____

Date: _____

"The right hand of the LORD exalts, the right hand of the LORD does valiantly!" (*Psalm 118:16*)

Dear God; Today I am most grateful for: ☀

What would make today a great day for me?

Today's Affirmation: I am...

What is the most amazing thing that happened today? ☾

_____
_____
_____
_____

How will I make tomorrow better?

_____
_____
_____
_____

Date: _____

"You are my hiding place and my shield; I hope in your word. Depart from me, you evildoers, that I may keep the commandments of my God." (Psalm 119:114-115)

Dear God; Today I am most grateful for:

What would make today a great day for me?

Today's Affirmation: I am...

What is the most amazing thing that happened today?

How will I make tomorrow better?

Date: _____

"This is my comfort in my affliction, that your promises give me life." *(Psalm 119:50)*

Dear God; Today I am most grateful for:

```
┌─────────────────────────────────────────────────────┐
│                                                       │
│                                                       │
│                                                       │
└─────────────────────────────────────────────────────┘
```

What would make today a great day for me?

```
┌─────────────────────────────────────────────────────┐
│                                                       │
│                                                       │
│                                                       │
└─────────────────────────────────────────────────────┘
```

Today's Affirmation: I am...

```
┌─────────────────────────────────────────────────────┐
│                                                       │
│                                                       │
│                                                       │
└─────────────────────────────────────────────────────┘
```

What is the most amazing thing that happened today?

How will I make tomorrow better?

Date: _____

Dear God; Today I am most grateful for:

What would make today a great day for me?

Today's Affirmation: I am...

What is the most amazing thing that happened today?

How will I make tomorrow better?

Date: _____

"You keep him in perfect peace whose mind is stayed on you, because he trusts in you."
(Isaiah 26:3)

Dear God; Today I am most grateful for:

```



```

What would make today a great day for me?

```



```

Today's Affirmation: I am...

```



```

What is the most amazing thing that happened today?

_____
_____
_____
_____

How will I make tomorrow better?

_____
_____
_____

Date: _____

"When you pass through the waters, I will be with you; through the rivers, they shall not overwhelm you; when you walk through fire you shall not be burned, the flame shall not consume you." (Isaiah 43:2)

Dear God; Today I am most grateful for:

```

```

What would make today a great day for me?

```

```

Today's Affirmation: I am...

```

```

What is the most amazing thing that happened today?

_____
_____
_____
_____

How will I make tomorrow better?

_____
_____
_____
_____

Date: _____

"Come to me, all who labor and are heavy laden, and I will give you rest."
(Matthew 11:28)

Dear God; Today I am most grateful for:

```

```

What would make today a great day for me?

```

```

Today's Affirmation: I am...

```

```

What is the most amazing thing that happened today?

_____
_____
_____
_____

How will I make tomorrow better?

_____
_____
_____
_____

Date: _____

"Jesus looked at them and said, with man it is impossible, but with God all things are possible." *(Mark 10:27)*

Dear God; Today I am most grateful for:

```



```

What would make today a great day for me?

```



```

Today's Affirmation: I am...

```



```

What is the most amazing thing that happened today?

_____

_____

_____

_____

How will I make tomorrow better?

_____

_____

_____

_____

Date: _____

"Be strong and courageous, follow the law that Moses commanded you. Do not turn from it to the or the left, that you may have good success wherever you go." (Joshua 1:7)

Dear God; Today I am most grateful for:

What would make today a great day for me?

Today's Affirmation: I am...

What is the most amazing thing that happened today?

_____

_____

_____

_____

How will I make tomorrow better?

_____

_____

_____

_____

Date: _____

"I have said these things to you, that in me you may have peace.
In the world you will have tribulation. But take heart; I have overcome the world."
(John 16:33)

Dear God; Today I am most grateful for:

What would make today a great day for me?

Today's Affirmation: I am...

What is the most amazing thing that happened today?

_____
_____
_____
_____

How will I make tomorrow better?

_____
_____
_____
_____

Date: _____

Dear God; Today I am most grateful for:

What would make today a great day for me?

Today's Affirmation: I am...

What is the most amazing thing that happened today?

_____
_____
_____
_____

How will I make tomorrow better?

_____
_____
_____
_____

Date: _____

"You have made us a little lower than the angels and crowned us with glory and honor, and put all things under our feet." **(Psalm 8:4 - 6)**

Dear God; Today I am most grateful for:

┌───┐
│   │
│   │
│   │
└───┘

What would make today a great day for me?

┌───┐
│   │
│   │
│   │
└───┘

Today's Affirmation: I am...

┌───┐
│   │
│   │
│   │
└───┘

What is the most amazing thing that happened today?

_____
_____
_____
_____

How will I make tomorrow better?

_____
_____
_____
_____

Date: _____

"Casting all your anxieties on him, because he cares for you." (1 Peter 5:7)

Dear God; Today I am most grateful for:

```
[                                                    ]
[                                                    ]
[                                                    ]
```

What would make today a great day for me?

```
[                                                    ]
[                                                    ]
[                                                    ]
```

Today's Affirmation: I am...

```
[                                                    ]
[                                                    ]
[                                                    ]
```

What is the most amazing thing that happened today?

_____
_____
_____
_____

How will I make tomorrow better?

_____
_____
_____
_____

Date: _____

"Be strong and courageous. Do not be afraid, for it is the LORD your God who goes with you. He will not leave you or forsake you." (Deuteronomy 31:6)

Dear God; Today I am most grateful for:

What would make today a great day for me?

Today's Affirmation: I am...

What is the most amazing thing that happened today?

How will I make tomorrow better?

Date: _____

"The LORD is good, a stronghold in the day of trouble; he knows those who take refuge in him."
(Nahum 1:7)

Dear God; Today I am most grateful for:

```
┌─────────────────────────────────────────────┐
│                                             │
│                                             │
│                                             │
└─────────────────────────────────────────────┘
```

What would make today a great day for me?

```
┌─────────────────────────────────────────────┐
│                                             │
│                                             │
│                                             │
└─────────────────────────────────────────────┘
```

Today's Affirmation: I am...

```
┌─────────────────────────────────────────────┐
│                                             │
│                                             │
│                                             │
└─────────────────────────────────────────────┘
```

What is the most amazing thing that happened today?

_____
_____
_____
_____

How will I make tomorrow better?

_____
_____
_____
_____

Date: _____

"One thing have I asked of the LORD, that will I seek after: that I may dwell in the house of the LORD all the days of my life." (Psalm 27:4)

Dear God; Today I am most grateful for:

What would make today a great day for me?

Today's Affirmation: I am...

What is the most amazing thing that happened today?

How will I make tomorrow better?

Date: _____

"Oh, taste and see that the LORD is good! Blessed is the man
who takes refuge in him!" (Psalm 34:8)

Dear God; Today I am most grateful for:

Today's Affirmation: I am...

What would make today a great day for me?

Today's Affirmation: I am...

What is the most amazing thing that happened today?

_____
_____
_____
_____

How will I make tomorrow better?

_____
_____
_____
_____

Date: _____

"A friend loves at all times, and a brother is born for adversity." (Proverbs 17:17)

Dear God; Today I am most grateful for:

```
┌─────────────────────────────────────────────┐
│                                               │
│                                               │
│                                               │
└─────────────────────────────────────────────┘
```

What would make today a great day for me?

```
┌─────────────────────────────────────────────┐
│                                               │
│                                               │
│                                               │
└─────────────────────────────────────────────┘
```

Today's Affirmation: I am...

```
┌─────────────────────────────────────────────┐
│                                               │
│                                               │
│                                               │
└─────────────────────────────────────────────┘
```

What is the most amazing thing that happened today?

_____
_____
_____
_____

How will I make tomorrow better?

_____
_____
_____
_____

Date: _____

"You keep him in perfect peace whose mind is stayed on you, because he trusts in you."
(Isaiah 26:3)

Dear God; Today I am most grateful for:

What would make today a great day for me?

Today's Affirmation: I am...

What is the most amazing thing that happened today?

_____
_____
_____
_____

How will I make tomorrow better?

_____
_____
_____
_____

Date: _____

"Greater love has no one than this, that a man lay down his life for his friends."
(John 15:13)

Dear God; Today I am most grateful for:

```



```

What would make today a great day for me?

```



```

Today's Affirmation: I am...

```



```

What is the most amazing thing that happened today?

_____
_____
_____
_____

How will I make tomorrow better?

_____
_____
_____
_____

Date: _____

"And we know that all things work together for the good, of those who love the Lord and are called according to his purpose." (*Romans 8:28*)

Dear God; Today I am most grateful for:

What would make today a great day for me?

Today's Affirmation: I am...

What is the most amazing thing that happened today?

_____
_____
_____
_____

How will I make tomorrow better?

_____
_____
_____
_____

Date: _____

"What then shall we say to these things? If God is for us, who can be against us?"
(Romans 8:31)

Dear God; Today I am most grateful for:

What would make today a great day for me?

Today's Affirmation: I am...

What is the most amazing thing that happened today?

How will I make tomorrow better?

Date: _____

"Nothing in all creation can separate us from the love of Christ Jesus our Lord. Not death nor life, angels or rulers, things present or things to come." (Romans 8:38-39)

Dear God; Today I am most grateful for:

```
┌─────────────────────────────────────────────┐
│                                               │
│                                               │
│                                               │
└─────────────────────────────────────────────┘
```

What would make today a great day for me?

```
┌─────────────────────────────────────────────┐
│                                               │
│                                               │
│                                               │
└─────────────────────────────────────────────┘
```

Today's Affirmation: I am...

```
┌─────────────────────────────────────────────┐
│                                               │
│                                               │
│                                               │
└─────────────────────────────────────────────┘
```

What is the most amazing thing that happened today?

_____
_____
_____
_____

How will I make tomorrow better?

_____
_____
_____
_____

Date: _____

Dear God; Today I am most grateful for:

What would make today a great day for me?

Today's Affirmation: I am...

What is the most amazing thing that happened today?

_____
_____
_____
_____

How will I make tomorrow better?

_____
_____
_____
_____

Date: _____

"For now, we see in a mirror dimly, but then face to face. Now I know in part; Then, I shall know fully, even as I have been fully known." (1 Corinthians 13:12)

Dear God; Today I am most grateful for:

What would make today a great day for me?

Today's Affirmation: I am...

What is the most amazing thing that happened today?

_____
_____
_____
_____

How will I make tomorrow better?

_____
_____
_____
_____

Date: _____

"Therefore, my beloved brothers, be steadfast, immovable, always abounding in the work of the Lord, knowing that in the Lord your labor is not in vain." (1 Corinthians 15:58)

Dear God; Today I am most grateful for:

What would make today a great day for me?

Today's Affirmation: I am...

What is the most amazing thing that happened today?

_____
_____
_____
_____

How will I make tomorrow better?

_____
_____
_____

Date: _____

"Be watchful, stand firm in the faith, act like men, be strong." (1 Corinthians 16:13)

Dear God; Today I am most grateful for:

_____

What would make today a great day for me?

_____

Today's Affirmation: I am...

_____

What is the most amazing thing that happened today?

_____
_____
_____
_____

How will I make tomorrow better?

_____
_____
_____
_____

Date: _____

*"But you are a chosen race, a royal priesthood, a holy nation,
a people for God's own possession."* **(1 Peter 2:9)**

Dear God; Today I am most grateful for:

What would make today a great day for me?

Today's Affirmation: I am...

What is the most amazing thing that happened today?

_____
_____
_____
_____

How will I make tomorrow better?

_____
_____
_____
_____

Date: _____

"Beloved, I urge you as sojourners and exiles to abstain from the passions of the flesh, which wage war against your soul." (1 Peter 2:11)

Dear God; Today I am most grateful for:

What would make today a great day for me?

Today's Affirmation: I am...

What is the most amazing thing that happened today?

_____
_____
_____
_____

How will I make tomorrow better?

_____
_____
_____
_____

Date: _____

"Count it all joy, when you have trials, for the testing of your faith produces steadfastness." (*James 1:2*)

Dear God; Today I am most grateful for:

What would make today a great day for me?

Today's Affirmation: I am...

What is the most amazing thing that happened today?

_____
_____
_____
_____

How will I make tomorrow better?

_____
_____
_____
_____

Date: _____

"And whatever we ask we receive from God, because we keep his commandments and do what pleases him." (1 John 3:22)

Dear God; Today I am most grateful for:

```



```

What would make today a great day for me?

```



```

Today's Affirmation: I am...

```



```

What is the most amazing thing that happened today? 🌙

_____

_____

_____

_____

How will I make tomorrow better?

_____

_____

_____

_____

Date: _____

"The LORD is my strength and my song, and he has become my salvation; this is my God, and I will praise him, and I will exalt him." **(Exodus 15:2)**

Dear God; Today I am most grateful for:

What would make today a great day for me?

Today's Affirmation: I am...

What is the most amazing thing that happened today?

How will I make tomorrow better?

Date: _____

"Both riches and honor come from you, and you rule over all. In your hands are power and might, in your hand, it is to make great and to give strength to all." **(1 Chronicles 29:12)**

Dear God; Today I am most grateful for:

What would make today a great day for me?

Today's Affirmation: I am...

What is the most amazing thing that happened today?

_____

_____

_____

_____

How will I make tomorrow better?

_____

_____

_____

_____

Date: _____

"Do not be grieved, for the joy of the LORD is your strength." (*Nehemiah 8:10*)

Dear God; Today I am most grateful for:

```
┌─────────────────────────────────────────────┐
│                                               │
│                                               │
│                                               │
│                                               │
└─────────────────────────────────────────────┘
```

What would make today a great day for me?

```
┌─────────────────────────────────────────────┐
│                                               │
│                                               │
│                                               │
│                                               │
└─────────────────────────────────────────────┘
```

Today's Affirmation: I am...

```
┌─────────────────────────────────────────────┐
│                                               │
│                                               │
│                                               │
│                                               │
└─────────────────────────────────────────────┘
```

What is the most amazing thing that happened today?

_____

_____

_____

_____

How will I make tomorrow better?

_____

_____

_____

_____

Date: _____

"Out of the mouth of babies and infants, you have established strength because of your foes, to still the enemy and the avenger." **(Psalm 8:2)**

Dear God; Today I am most grateful for:

```



```

What would make today a great day for me?

```



```

Today's Affirmation: I am...

```



```

What is the most amazing thing that happened today?

_____
_____
_____
_____

How will I make tomorrow better?

_____
_____
_____
_____

Date: _____

"I love you, O LORD, my strength." **(Psalm 18:1)**

Dear God; Today I am most grateful for:

What would make today a great day for me?

Today's Affirmation: I am...

What is the most amazing thing that happened today?

_____
_____
_____
_____

How will I make tomorrow better?

_____
_____
_____
_____

Date: _____

"The LORD is my rock and my fortress and my deliverer, my God, in whom I take refuge, my shield, and the horn of my salvation, my stronghold." **(Psalm 18:2)**

Dear God; Today I am most grateful for:

What would make today a great day for me?

Today's Affirmation: I am...

What is the most amazing thing that happened today?

_____
_____
_____
_____

How will I make tomorrow better?

_____
_____
_____
_____

Date: _____

"The LORD is my light and my salvation; whom shall I fear?
The LORD is the strength of my life; of whom shall I be afraid?" **(Psalm 27:1)**

Dear God; Today I am most grateful for:

What would make today a great day for me?

Today's Affirmation: I am...

What is the most amazing thing that happened today?

_____
_____
_____
_____

How will I make tomorrow better?

_____
_____
_____
_____

Date: _____

"Blessed is the one who trusts in the LORD." **(Jeremiah 17:7)**

Dear God; Today I am most grateful for:

```



```

What would make today a great day for me?

```



```

Today's Affirmation: I am...

```



```

What is the most amazing thing that happened today?

_____
_____
_____
_____

How will I make tomorrow better?

_____
_____
_____
_____

Date: _____

"Give ear to my words, o Lord, consider my meditation." **(Psalm 5:1)**

Dear God; Today I am most grateful for:

```



```

What would make today a great day for me?

```



```

Today's Affirmation: I am...

```



```

What is the most amazing thing that happened today?

_____

_____

_____

_____

How will I make tomorrow better?

_____

_____

_____

_____

Date: _____

"The salvation of the righteous is from the LORD;
He is their stronghold in the time of trouble." **(Psalm 37:39)**

Dear God; Today I am most grateful for:

What would make today a great day for me?

Today's Affirmation: I am...

What is the most amazing thing that happened today?

How will I make tomorrow better?

Date: _____

"God is our refuge and strength, an ever-present help in trouble." (Psalm 46:1)

Dear God; Today I am most grateful for: ☀

```
┌─────────────────────────────────────────────────────────┐
│                                                           │
│                                                           │
│                                                           │
└─────────────────────────────────────────────────────────┘
```

What would make today a great day for me?

```
┌─────────────────────────────────────────────────────────┐
│                                                           │
│                                                           │
│                                                           │
└─────────────────────────────────────────────────────────┘
```

Today's Affirmation: I am...

```
┌─────────────────────────────────────────────────────────┐
│                                                           │
│                                                           │
│                                                           │
└─────────────────────────────────────────────────────────┘
```

What is the most amazing thing that happened today? ☾

_____
_____
_____
_____

How will I make tomorrow better?

_____
_____
_____
_____

Date: _____

Dear God; Today I am most grateful for:

```


```

What would make today a great day for me?

```


```

Today's Affirmation: I am...

```


```

What is the most amazing thing that happened today?

_____
_____
_____
_____

How will I make tomorrow better?

_____
_____
_____
_____

Date: _____

"My soul melts away for sorrow; strengthen me according to your word!" **(Psalm 119:28)**

Dear God; Today I am most grateful for:

What would make today a great day for me?

Today's Affirmation: I am...

What is the most amazing thing that happened today?

How will I make tomorrow better?

Date: _____

"When I called, you answered me; you greatly emboldened me." **(Psalm 138:3)**

Dear God; Today I am most grateful for:

```
┌──────────────────────────────────────────────┐
│                                              │
│                                              │
│                                              │
│                                              │
└──────────────────────────────────────────────┘
```

What would make today a great day for me?

```
┌──────────────────────────────────────────────┐
│                                              │
│                                              │
│                                              │
│                                              │
└──────────────────────────────────────────────┘
```

Today's Affirmation: I am...

```
┌──────────────────────────────────────────────┐
│                                              │
│                                              │
│                                              │
│                                              │
└──────────────────────────────────────────────┘
```

What is the most amazing thing that happened today?

_____
_____
_____
_____

How will I make tomorrow better?

_____
_____
_____
_____

Date: _____

"God is my salvation; I will trust, and will not be afraid; for the LORD GOD is my strength and song, and he has become my salvation." **(Isaiah 12:2)**

Dear God; Today I am most grateful for:

What would make today a great day for me?

Today's Affirmation: I am...

What is the most amazing thing that happened today?

_____
_____
_____
_____

How will I make tomorrow better?

_____
_____
_____
_____

Date: _____

"The Lord, is my strength; he makes my feet like the deer's;
He makes me to tread on high places." (Habakkuk 3:19)

Dear God; Today I am most grateful for:

What would make today a great day for me?

Today's Affirmation: I am...

What is the most amazing thing that happened today?

How will I make tomorrow better?

Date: _____

Dear God; Today I am most grateful for:

What would make today a great day for me?

Today's Affirmation: I am...

What is the most amazing thing that happened today?

_____
_____
_____
_____

How will I make tomorrow better?

_____
_____
_____
_____

Date: _____

"Jesus looked at them and said, 'With man this is impossible, but with God all things are possible." (Matthew 19:26)

Dear God; Today I am most grateful for:

[ ]

What would make today a great day for me?

[ ]

Today's Affirmation: I am...

[ ]

What is the most amazing thing that happened today?

_____
_____
_____
_____

How will I make tomorrow better?

_____
_____
_____
_____

Date: _____

"You shall love the Lord your God with all your heart and with all your soul and with all your mind and with all your strength." **(Mark 12:30)**

Dear God; Today I am most grateful for:

What would make today a great day for me?

Today's Affirmation: I am...

What is the most amazing thing that happened today?

How will I make tomorrow better?

Date: _____

"You will receive power when the Holy Spirit has come upon you, and you will be my witnesses, throughout the world." (Acts 1:8)

Dear God; Today I am most grateful for:

What would make today a great day for me?

Today's Affirmation: I am...

What is the most amazing thing that happened today?

_____
_____
_____
_____

How will I make tomorrow better?

_____
_____
_____
_____

Date: _____

"We do not lose heart; Though our outer self is wasting away,
our inner self is being renewed day by day." **(2 Corinthians 4:16)**

Dear God; Today I am most grateful for:

```
┌─────────────────────────────────────────────┐
│                                             │
│                                             │
│                                             │
└─────────────────────────────────────────────┘
```

What would make today a great day for me?

```
┌─────────────────────────────────────────────┐
│                                             │
│                                             │
│                                             │
└─────────────────────────────────────────────┘
```

Today's Affirmation: I am...

```
┌─────────────────────────────────────────────┐
│                                             │
│                                             │
│                                             │
└─────────────────────────────────────────────┘
```

What is the most amazing thing that happened today?

_____
_____
_____
_____

How will I make tomorrow better?

_____
_____
_____
_____

Date: _____

"My grace is sufficient for you, for my power is made perfect in weakness."
(2 Corinthians 12:9)

Dear God; Today I am most grateful for:

What would make today a great day for me?

Today's Affirmation: I am...

What is the most amazing thing that happened today?

How will I make tomorrow better?

Date: _____

"I am content with weaknesses, insults, hardships, persecutions, and calamities.
For when I am weak, then I am strong." (2 Corinthians 12:10)

Dear God; Today I am most grateful for:

What would make today a great day for me?

Today's Affirmation: I am...

What is the most amazing thing that happened today?

_____
_____
_____
_____

How will I make tomorrow better?

_____
_____
_____
_____

Date: _____

"That according to the riches of his glory he may grant you to be strengthened with power through his Spirit in your inner being." **(Ephesians 3:16)**

Dear God; Today I am most grateful for:

What would make today a great day for me?

Today's Affirmation: I am...

What is the most amazing thing that happened today?

_____
_____
_____
_____

How will I make tomorrow better?

_____
_____
_____
_____

Date: _____

"I can do all things through him who strengthens me." **(Philippians 4:13)**

Dear God; Today I am most grateful for:

```



```

What would make today a great day for me?

```



```

Today's Affirmation: I am...

```



```

What is the most amazing thing that happened today?

_____
_____
_____
_____

How will I make tomorrow better?

_____
_____
_____
_____

Date: _____

"For God did not give us a spirit of fear, but of power, love and self-control."
(2 Timothy 1:7)

Dear God; Today I am most grateful for:

```


```

What would make today a great day for me?

```


```

Today's Affirmation: I am...

```


```

What is the most amazing thing that happened today?

_____
_____
_____
_____

How will I make tomorrow better?

_____
_____
_____
_____

Date: _____

"Fear not, for I am with you; be not dismayed, for I am your God; I will strengthen you, I will help you, I will uphold you with my righteous right hand." (Isaiah 41:10)

Dear God; Today I am most grateful for:

What would make today a great day for me?

Today's Affirmation: I am...

What is the most amazing thing that happened today?

How will I make tomorrow better?

Date: _____

"Those who wait for the Lord shall renew their strength; they shall mount up with wings like eagles; they shall run, and not be weary; they shall walk, and not faint."
(Isaiah 40:31)

Dear God; Today I am most grateful for:

What would make today a great day for me?

Today's Affirmation: I am...

What is the most amazing thing that happened today?

_____
_____
_____
_____

How will I make tomorrow better?

_____
_____
_____
_____

Date: _____

Dear God; Today I am most grateful for:

What would make today a great day for me?

Today's Affirmation: I am...

What is the most amazing thing that happened today?

How will I make tomorrow better?

Date: _____

"Be strong in the Lord and in the strength of his might." (*Ephesians 6:10*)

Dear God; Today I am most grateful for:

What would make today a great day for me?

Today's Affirmation: I am...

What is the most amazing thing that happened today?

_____
_____
_____
_____

How will I make tomorrow better?

_____
_____
_____
_____

Date: _____

Dear God; Today I am most grateful for:

What would make today a great day for me?

Today's Affirmation: I am...

What is the most amazing thing that happened today?

_____
_____
_____
_____

How will I make tomorrow better?

_____
_____
_____
_____

Date: _____

Today I am most grateful for:

What would make today a great day for me?

Today's Affirmation: I am...

What is the most amazing thing that happened today?

_____
_____
_____
_____

How will I make tomorrow better?

_____
_____
_____
_____

Date: _____

"So now faith, hope, and love abide, these three; but the greatest of these is love."
(1 Corinthians 13:13)

Dear God; Today I am most grateful for:

```


```

What would make today a great day for me?

```


```

Today's Affirmation: I am...

```


```

What is the most amazing thing that happened today?

_____
_____
_____
_____

How will I make tomorrow better?

_____
_____
_____
_____

Date: _____

"A new commandment I give to you, that you love one another: just as I have loved you, you also are to love one another. By this all people will know that you are my disciples, if you have love for one another." (*John 13:34-35*)

Dear God; Today I am most grateful for:

What would make today a great day for me?

Today's Affirmation: I am...

What is the most amazing thing that happened today?

_____
_____
_____
_____

How will I make tomorrow better?

_____
_____
_____
_____

Date: _____

"For it is with your hearth that you believe and are justified, and it is with your mouth that You profess your faith and are saved." (Romans 10:10)

Dear God; Today I am most grateful for:

What would make today a great day for me?

Today's Affirmation: I am...

What is the most amazing thing that happened today?

_____
_____
_____
_____

How will I make tomorrow better?

_____
_____
_____
_____

Date: _____

"Without faith it is impossible to please him, for whoever would draw near to God must believe that he exists and that he rewards those who seek him." (Hebrews 11:6)

Dear God; Today I am most grateful for:

What would make today a great day for me?

Today's Affirmation: I am...

What is the most amazing thing that happened today?

_____
_____
_____
_____

How will I make tomorrow better?

_____
_____
_____
_____

Date: _____

"Love is patient and kind; love does not envy or boast; it is not arrogant."
(1 Corinthians 13:4)

Dear God; Today I am most grateful for:

```



```

What would make today a great day for me?

```



```

Today's Affirmation: I am...

```



```

What is the most amazing thing that happened today?

_____
_____
_____
_____

How will I make tomorrow better?

_____
_____
_____
_____

Date: _____

"Now faith is the assurance of things hoped for, the conviction of things not seen."
(Hebrews 11:1)

Dear God; Today I am most grateful for:

What would make today a great day for me?

Today's Affirmation: I am...

What is the most amazing thing that happened today?

_____
_____
_____
_____

How will I make tomorrow better?

_____
_____
_____
_____

Date: _____

"Whatever you ask in prayer, believe that you have received it, and it will be yours."
(Mark 11:24)

Dear God; Today I am most grateful for:

```
┌─────────────────────────────────────────────┐
│                                               │
│                                               │
│                                               │
└─────────────────────────────────────────────┘
```

What would make today a great day for me?

```
┌─────────────────────────────────────────────┐
│                                               │
│                                               │
│                                               │
└─────────────────────────────────────────────┘
```

Today's Affirmation: I am...

```
┌─────────────────────────────────────────────┐
│                                               │
│                                               │
│                                               │
└─────────────────────────────────────────────┘
```

What is the most amazing thing that happened today?

_____
_____
_____
_____

How will I make tomorrow better?

_____
_____
_____
_____

Date: _____

"For nothing will be impossible with God." (Luke 1:37)

Dear God; Today I am most grateful for:

What would make today a great day for me?

Today's Affirmation: I am...

What is the most amazing thing that happened today?

_____
_____
_____
_____

How will I make tomorrow better?

_____
_____
_____
_____

Date: _____

"For by grace you have been saved through faith. And this is not your own doing; it is the gift of God, not a result of works, so that no one may boast." (Ephesians 2:8-9)

Dear God; Today I am most grateful for:

What would make today a great day for me?

Today's Affirmation: I am...

What is the most amazing thing that happened today?

_____

_____

_____

_____

How will I make tomorrow better?

_____

_____

_____

_____

Date: _____

Dear God; Today I am most grateful for:

What would make today a great day for me?

Today's Affirmation: I am...

What is the most amazing thing that happened today?

How will I make tomorrow better?

Date: _____

"For we walk by faith, not by sight." **(Corinthians 5:7)**

Dear God; Today I am most grateful for:

```
┌─────────────────────────────────────────────┐
│                                               │
│                                               │
│                                               │
└─────────────────────────────────────────────┘
```

What would make today a great day for me?

```
┌─────────────────────────────────────────────┐
│                                               │
│                                               │
│                                               │
└─────────────────────────────────────────────┘
```

Today's Affirmation: I am...

```
┌─────────────────────────────────────────────┐
│                                               │
│                                               │
│                                               │
└─────────────────────────────────────────────┘
```

What is the most amazing thing that happened today?

_____
_____
_____
_____

How will I make tomorrow better?

_____
_____
_____
_____

Date: _____

"Peace I leave with you; my peace I give to you. Not as the world gives, do I give to you. Let not your heart be troubled, neither let it be afraid." (John 14:27)

Dear God; Today I am most grateful for:

```



```

What would make today a great day for me?

```



```

Today's Affirmation: I am...

```



```

What is the most amazing thing that happened today?

_____
_____
_____
_____

How will I make tomorrow better?

_____
_____
_____
_____

Date: _____

"May the God of hope fill you with all joy and peace in believing, so that by the power of the Holy Spirit you may abound in hope." (Romans 15:13)

Dear God; Today I am most grateful for:

Where would make today a great day for me?

What would make today a great day for me?

Today's Affirmation: I am...

What is the most amazing thing that happened today?

_____
_____
_____
_____

How will I make tomorrow better?

_____
_____
_____
_____

Date: _____

"Rejoice in hope, be patient in tribulation, be constant in prayer." (Romans 12:12)

Dear God; Today I am most grateful for:

```
┌─────────────────────────────────────────────────────┐
│                                                       │
│                                                       │
│                                                       │
│                                                       │
└─────────────────────────────────────────────────────┘
```

What would make today a great day for me?

```
┌─────────────────────────────────────────────────────┐
│                                                       │
│                                                       │
│                                                       │
│                                                       │
└─────────────────────────────────────────────────────┘
```

Today's Affirmation: I am...

```
┌─────────────────────────────────────────────────────┐
│                                                       │
│                                                       │
│                                                       │
│                                                       │
└─────────────────────────────────────────────────────┘
```

What is the most amazing thing that happened today?

_____
_____
_____
_____

How will I make tomorrow better?

_____
_____
_____
_____

Date: _____

"Count it all joy, when you meet trials of various kinds." Because the testing of your faith produces perseverance." (James 1:2)

Dear God; Today I am most grateful for:

```
┌────────────────────────────────────────┐
│                                        │
│                                        │
│                                        │
└────────────────────────────────────────┘
```

What would make today a great day for me?

```
┌────────────────────────────────────────┐
│                                        │
│                                        │
│                                        │
└────────────────────────────────────────┘
```

Today's Affirmation: I am...

```
┌────────────────────────────────────────┐
│                                        │
│                                        │
│                                        │
└────────────────────────────────────────┘
```

What is the most amazing thing that happened today?

_____
_____
_____
_____

How will I make tomorrow better?

_____
_____
_____
_____

Date: _____

"Rejoice in the Lord always; again, I will say, Rejoice." (Philippians 4:4)

Dear God; Today I am most grateful for:

What would make today a great day for me?

Today's Affirmation: I am...

What is the most amazing thing that happened today?

_____
_____
_____
_____

How will I make tomorrow better?

_____
_____
_____
_____

Date: _____

"The fruit of the Spirit is love, joy, peace, patience, kindness, goodness, faithfulness." (Galatians 5:22)

Dear God; Today I am most grateful for:

What would make today a great day for me?

Today's Affirmation: I am...

What is the most amazing thing that happened today?

How will I make tomorrow better?

Date: _____

"Ask, and you will receive, that your joy may be full." (*John 6:24*)

Dear God; Today I am most grateful for:

```
┌────────────────────────────────────────────┐
│                                            │
│                                            │
│                                            │
└────────────────────────────────────────────┘
```

What would make today a great day for me?

```
┌────────────────────────────────────────────┐
│                                            │
│                                            │
│                                            │
└────────────────────────────────────────────┘
```

Today's Affirmation: I am...

```
┌────────────────────────────────────────────┐
│                                            │
│                                            │
│                                            │
└────────────────────────────────────────────┘
```

What is the most amazing thing that happened today?

_____
_____
_____
_____

How will I make tomorrow better?

_____
_____
_____
_____

Date: _____

"A joyful heart is good medicine, but a crushed spirit dries up the bones."
(Proverbs 17:22)

Dear God; Today I am most grateful for:

What would make today a great day for me?

Today's Affirmation: I am...

What is the most amazing thing that happened today?

How will I make tomorrow better?

2 Corinthians 5:7
For I walk by faith,
not by sight

Date: _____

"Though you have not seen him, you love him. Though you do not now see him, you believe in him and rejoice with joy that is inexpressible and filled with glory." (1 Peter 1:8)

Dear God; Today I am most grateful for:

[ ]

What would make today a great day for me?

[ ]

Today's Affirmation: I am...

[ ]

What is the most amazing thing that happened today?

_____
_____
_____
_____

How will I make tomorrow better?

_____
_____
_____
_____

Date: _____

"So also, you have sorrow now, but I will see you again, and your hearts will rejoice, and no one will take your joy from you." (**John 16:22**)

Dear God; Today I am most grateful for:

> [ ]

What would make today a great day for me?

> [ ]

Today's Affirmation: I am...

> [ ]

What is the most amazing thing that happened today?

_____
_____
_____
_____

How will I make tomorrow better?

_____
_____
_____
_____

Date: _____

"My God will meet all your needs according to the riches of his glory in Christ Jesus."
(Philippians 4:19)

Dear God; Today I am most grateful for:

[ ]

What would make today a great day for me?

[ ]

Today's Affirmation: I am...

[ ]

What is the most amazing thing that happened today?

_____
_____
_____
_____

How will I make tomorrow better?

_____
_____
_____
_____

Date: _____

"The Lord is my shepherd, I shall not want." (Psalm 23:1)

Dear God; Today I am most grateful for: ☀

What would make today a great day for me?

Today's Affirmation: I am...

What is the most amazing thing that happened today? ☽

_____
_____
_____
_____

How will I make tomorrow better?

_____
_____
_____
_____

Date: _____

"My God is my rock, in whom, I take refuge, my shield and the horn of my salvation."
(2 Samuel 22:3)

Today I am most grateful for:

What would make today a great day for me?

Today's Affirmation: I am...

What is the most amazing thing that happened today?

_____
_____
_____
_____

How will I make tomorrow better?

_____
_____
_____
_____

Date: _____

"Though I walk in the midst of trouble, you preserve my life. You stretch out your hand against the anger of my foes; with your right hand you save me." (Psalm 138:7)

Today I am most grateful for:

What would make today a great day for me?

Today's Affirmation: I am...

What is the most amazing thing that happened today?

_____
_____
_____
_____

How will I make tomorrow better?

_____
_____
_____
_____

Date: _____

Faith comes from hearing, hearing the word of Christ." (*Romans* 10:17)

Dear God; Today I am most grateful for:

_____

What would make today a great day for me?

_____

Today's Affirmation: I am...

_____

What is the most amazing thing that happened today?

_____

How will I make tomorrow better?

_____

Date: _____

"Commit to the Lord whatever you do, and he will establish your plans." (Proverbs 16:3)

Dear God; Today I am most grateful for:

| |
| |

What would make today a great day for me?

| |
| |

Today's Affirmation: I am...

| |
| |

What is the most amazing thing that happened today?

_____
_____
_____
_____

How will I make tomorrow better?

_____
_____
_____
_____

Date: _____

Dear God; Today I am most grateful for:

What would make today a great day for me?

Today's Affirmation: I am...

What is the most amazing thing that happened today?

_____
_____
_____
_____

How will I make tomorrow better?

_____
_____
_____
_____

Date: _____

"My spirit rejoices in God my Savior." (Luke 1:47)

Dear God; Today I am most grateful for:

What would make today a great day for me?

Today's Affirmation: I am...

What is the most amazing thing that happened today?

_____
_____
_____
_____

How will I make tomorrow better?

_____
_____
_____
_____

Date: _____

"Worship the Lord your God, and his blessing will be on your food and water. And he will take away sickness from among you." (Exodus 23:25)

Today I am most grateful for:

What would make today a great day for me?

Today's Affirmation: I am...

What is the most amazing thing that happened today?

_____
_____
_____
_____

How will I make tomorrow better?

_____
_____
_____
_____

Date: _____

"For I know the plans I have for you, declares the Lord, plans to prosper you and not to harm you, plans to give you hope and a future." **(Jeremiah 29:11)**

Today I am most grateful for:

What would make today a great day for me?

Today's Affirmation: I am...

What is the most amazing thing that happened today?

How will I make tomorrow better?

Date: _____

"Bless those who persecute you; bless and do not curse." (*Romans* 12:14)

Dear God; Today I am most grateful for:

```
┌─────────────────────────────────────────────┐
│                                             │
│                                             │
│                                             │
└─────────────────────────────────────────────┘
```

What would make today a great day for me?

```
┌─────────────────────────────────────────────┐
│                                             │
│                                             │
│                                             │
└─────────────────────────────────────────────┘
```

Today's Affirmation: I am...

```
┌─────────────────────────────────────────────┐
│                                             │
│                                             │
│                                             │
└─────────────────────────────────────────────┘
```

What is the most amazing thing that happened today?

_____
_____
_____
_____

How will I make tomorrow better?

_____
_____
_____
_____

Date: _____

"The grace of the Lord Jesus Christ be with your spirit, Amen." **(Philemon 1:25)**

Dear God; Today I am most grateful for:

What would make today a great day for me?

Today's Affirmation: I am...

What is the most amazing thing that happened today?

_____
_____
_____
_____

How will I make tomorrow better?

_____
_____
_____
_____

Date: _____

"Blessed are the peacemakers, for they will be called children of God."
(Matthew 5:9)

Dear God; Today I am most grateful for: ☀

What would make today a great day for me?

Today's Affirmation: I am...

What is the most amazing thing that happened today? ☽

_____
_____
_____
_____

How could I have made today better?

_____
_____
_____
_____

Date: _____

"The grace of the Lord Jesus Christ be with your spirit. Amen."
(Philippians 4:23)

Dear God; Today I am most grateful for:

What would make today a great day for me?

Today's Affirmation: I am...

What is the most amazing thing that happened today?

How could I have made today better?

Date: _____

"Every good gift and every perfect gift comes from above, and comes down from the Father of lights, with whom there is no fickleness, neither shadow of turning." (**James 1:17**)

Dear God; Today I am most grateful for:

What would make today a great day for me?

Today's Affirmation: I am...

What is the most amazing thing that happened today?

How will I make tomorrow better?

Date: _____

"For it is by grace you have been saved, through faith, and this is not from yourselves, it is the gift of God." (Ephesians 2:8)

Dear God; Today I am most grateful for:

What would make today a great day for me?

Today's Affirmation: I am...

What is the most amazing thing that happened today?

_____
_____
_____
_____

How will I make tomorrow better?

_____
_____
_____
_____

Date: _____

Dear God; Today I am most grateful for:

What would make today a great day for me?

Today's Affirmation: I am...

What is the most amazing thing that happened today?

_____

_____

_____

_____

How will I make tomorrow better?

_____

_____

_____

_____

Date: _____

"Whoever pursues righteousness and love, finds life, prosperity and honor."
(Proverbs 21:21)

Dear God; Today I am most grateful for:

What would make today a great day for me?

Today's Affirmation: I am...

What is the most amazing thing that happened today?

How will I make tomorrow better?

Date: _____

"As water reflects the face, so one's life reflects the heart."
(Proverbs 27:19)

Dear God; Today I am most grateful for:

What would make today a great day for me?

Today's Affirmation: I am...

What is the most amazing thing that happened today?

_____
_____
_____
_____

How will I make tomorrow better?

_____
_____
_____
_____

Date: _____

"Show me your ways, Lord, teach me your paths."
(Psalm 25:4)

Dear God; Today I am most grateful for:

What would make today a great day for me?

Today's Affirmation: I am...

What is the most amazing thing that happened today?

_____
_____
_____
_____

How will I make tomorrow better?

_____
_____
_____
_____

Date: _____

"Then Jesus declared, "I am the bread of life. Whoever comes to me will never go hungry, and whoever believes in me will never be thirsty." **(John 6:35)**

Dear God; Today I am most grateful for:

What would make today a great day for me?

Today's Affirmation: I am...

What is the most amazing thing that happened today?

_____
_____
_____
_____

How will I make tomorrow better?

_____
_____
_____
_____

Date: _____

"Surely your goodness and love will follow me all the days of my life, and I will dwell in the house of the Lord forever." **(Psalm 23:6)**

Dear God; Today I am most grateful for:

What would make today a great day for me?

Today's Affirmation: I am...

What is the most amazing thing that happened today?

_____
_____
_____
_____

How will I make tomorrow better?

_____
_____
_____
_____

Date: _____

"Make every effort to live in peace with everyone and to be holy; without holiness no one will see the Lord." (Hebrews 12:14)

Dear God; Today I am most grateful for:

```
┌─────────────────────────────────────────────────────────┐
│                                                         │
│                                                         │
│                                                         │
│                                                         │
└─────────────────────────────────────────────────────────┘
```

What would make today a great day for me?

```
┌─────────────────────────────────────────────────────────┐
│                                                         │
│                                                         │
│                                                         │
│                                                         │
└─────────────────────────────────────────────────────────┘
```

Today's Affirmation: I am...

```
┌─────────────────────────────────────────────────────────┐
│                                                         │
│                                                         │
│                                                         │
│                                                         │
└─────────────────────────────────────────────────────────┘
```

What is the most amazing thing that happened today?

_____
_____
_____
_____

How will I make tomorrow better?

_____
_____
_____
_____

Date: _____

"And the peace of God, which transcends all understanding, will guard your hearts and minds in Christ Jesus." (Philippians 4:7)

Dear God; Today I am most grateful for:

What would make today a great day for me?

Today's Affirmation: I am...

What is the most amazing thing that happened today?

_____
_____
_____
_____

How will I make tomorrow better?

_____
_____
_____
_____

Date: _____

"Blessed are the pure in heart, for they will see God."
(Ephesians 1:11)

Dear God; Today I am most grateful for: ☀

┌───┐
│   │
│   │
│   │
└───┘

What would make today a great day for me?

┌───┐
│   │
│   │
│   │
└───┘

Today's Affirmation: I am...

┌───┐
│   │
│   │
│   │
└───┘

What is the most amazing thing that happened today? ☾

_____
_____
_____
_____

How will I make tomorrow better?

_____
_____
_____
_____

Date: _____

For his anger lasts only a moment, but his favor lasts a lifetime; weeping may stay for the night, but rejoicing comes in the morning." (Psalm 30:5)

Dear God; Today I am most grateful for:

What would make today a great day for me?

Today's Affirmation: I am...

What is the most amazing thing that happened today?

How will I make tomorrow better?

Date: _____

"Seek first his kingdom and his righteousness and all things will be given to you."
(Matthew 6:33)

Dear God; Today I am most grateful for:

What would make today a great day for me?

Today's Affirmation: I am...

What is the most amazing thing that happened today?

_____
_____
_____
_____

How will I make tomorrow better?

_____
_____
_____
_____

Date: _____

"Surely, LORD, you bless the righteous; you surround them with your favor as with a shield." (Psalm 5:12)

Dear God; Today I am most grateful for: ✴

What would make today a great day for me?

Today's Affirmation: I am...

What is the most amazing thing that happened today? 🌙

_____
_____
_____
_____

How will I make tomorrow better?

_____
_____
_____
_____

Date: _____

"The angel went to her and said, "Greetings, you who are highly favored! The Lord is with you." (Luke 1:28)

Dear God; Today I am most grateful for:

What would make today a great day for me?

Today's Affirmation: I am...

What is the most amazing thing that happened today?

_____
_____
_____
_____

How will I make tomorrow better?

_____
_____
_____
_____

Psalm 46:1-2
God is my refuge and
strength,
an ever present help in
trouble;
Therefore, I will not
fear.

Ideas For Selfcare

- ✓ Take a mental health day, and do not feel an ounce of guilt about it
- ✓ Burn a candle or diffuse some oils that have scents that bring you joy
- ✓ Walk around the grocery store without a list; Buy some stuff just for fun
- ✓ Go to the library or bookstore; Sit in a comfy chair and read
- ✓ Sing at the top of your lungs, in the car, with the windows down
- ✓ Do something crafty: coloring, knitting, sewing.....
- ✓ Take a bubble bath with candles and calming music
- ✓ Sit in a coffee shop and sip on a luxurious drink
- ✓ Sit on the front porch; Just sit and do nothing
- ✓ Sit in the grass and watch the clouds float by
- ✓ Pick or buy a bouquet of fresh flowers
- ✓ Go for a drive - no destination required
- ✓ Have a dance party to your favorite music
- ✓ Wrap yourself in a soft, warm blanket
- ✓ Give yourself a pedicure or a manicure
- ✓ Read a book or magazine for an hour
- ✓ Take a leisurely walk without a goal
- ✓ Put on a homemade face mask
- ✓ Watch funny YouTube videos
- ✓ Try out a new hobby
- ✓ Look at the stars
- ✓ Sit in the sun
- ✓ Meditate
- ✓ Take a nap
- ✓ Write in your Journal

My Reflections:

_____
_____
_____
_____
_____
_____
_____
_____
_____
_____
_____
_____
_____
_____
_____
_____
_____

My Reflections:

My Reflections:

Inspiration

As a Christian woman there are so many wonderful moments that I have experienced with The Lord that have caused me to rejoice and to be filled with hope for the future, no matter what I am going through. I often recount these moments to others; including my children, family members, friends and church family. I realized it would have been so much easier to recount some of these experiences to uplift the people that I am talking to by reading from my journals instead of trying to remember all the details from memory.

I created this journal, to help my fellow believers around the world to be embolden to document and share their encounters with God and proudly capture his greatness. This will help you to pass on great inspirational stories and spiritual traditions to the next generation and to encourage you to bring others into the presence of God.

My hope is that this journal will encourage you to record your thoughts and beliefs, to record those inspirational moments that have helped to bring you closer to the Lord and also to develop within you an attitude of gratitude and praise for all the wonderful miracles that God has worked in your life.

Deuteronomy 7:9 - Know therefore that the LORD your God is God; he is the faithful God, keeping his covenant of love to a thousand generations of those who love him and keep his commandments.

-A.R. Francis

Made in the USA
Coppell, TX
10 December 2021

67991346R00075